What Are Sharks?

Sharks are fish that live in the sea. There have been sharks in the sea for millions of years. The smallest sharks are the size of a human hand. The biggest sharks are bigger than a bus!

Shark skin
up close

Sharks have gills, fins and scales. The scales on their skin are rough, like sandpaper. Sharks have no bones in their body. They have cartilage. Cartilage is softer than bone, but it is very strong.

4

SHARKS

Jillian Powell

RIGBY

Contents

What Are Sharks? 3

A Shark's Life 6

How Sharks Swim 10

Sharks and People 14

Amazing Sharks 18

Shark Facts 22

Index 24

Sharks swim in seas
all over the world.

Fish Facts

- All fish live and breathe in water.
- All fish breathe with gills.
- All fish have fins.
- Most fish have scales on their skin.
- Most fish have bones in their body.
- Most fish lay eggs.
- Some fish give birth to live babies.

A Shark's Life

Most sharks give birth to live babies. Their babies are called pups. Some sharks give birth to about 100 pups at a time. The pups can swim and hunt for food as soon as they are born.

Lemon sharks give birth to live babies.

Swell sharks hatch from eggs.

Others kinds of sharks lay eggs. They lay their eggs down on the bottom of the sea. Baby sharks hatch from the eggs. All baby sharks grow to their full size in 10 to 15 years.

Sharks eat other fish and sea animals. They can smell, hear and even feel animals in the water.

Most sharks have about 5 rows of teeth. They use their teeth to catch other fish and sea animals. The biggest teeth are at the front of a shark's mouth. When one of these teeth falls out, a new tooth moves up into its place.

Some sharks have 3000 teeth.

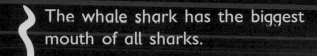

The whale shark has the biggest mouth of all sharks.

Whale sharks are different. They eat only small fish and tiny living things called plankton. A whale shark swims with its mouth open. The small fish and plankton go into the shark's open mouth.

How Sharks Swim

Most sharks swim almost all the time. They can swim a long way. The shape of a shark's body helps it to move through the water.

A shark's fin helps it turn in the water.

Angel sharks hide on the bottom of the sea.

Sharks use their tail to move forward in the water. They use their fins to swim up or down. The fin on their back helps them to turn.

Some sharks don't swim very much. These sharks live down on the bottom of the sea. They are flat, so they can hide in the sand!

Most sharks swim alone. But some sharks swim in groups called schools. Thousands of sharks can swim in one school under the sea.

Hammerhead sharks swim in schools.

Some sharks stay where they are born. Other sharks swim thousands of miles every year. They swim all that way to find food.

Bull sharks swim more than 2,000 miles every year.

Sharks and People

Some sharks are killed by people. People kill sharks for their meat, fins and teeth. Other sharks die because they get trapped in fishing nets.

Shark fins are used for food.

A shark trapped in a fishing net.

Some kinds of sharks are in danger of dying out because too many of them have been killed. There are only a few great white sharks left in the world. In some places, people have been stopped from killing them.

The most dangerous sharks are the great white sharks. They sometimes attack people. The sharks think people are seals, which they like to eat!

A great white shark hunting a seal.

Many people are afraid of sharks. But sharks kill very few humans. There are only about 100 attacks on people every year. Pigs kill more people every year than sharks do!

Amazing Sharks

There were sharks long before there were dinosaurs. The first sharks lived about 400 million years ago. Today, there are more than 350 kinds of sharks.

The first sharks had teeth as big as a human hand.

Sharks live in seas all over the world. But the sea near Costa Rica has more sharks than any other place.

A white-tip reef shark near Costa Rica.

A blue shark.

The blue shark is one of the fastest sharks. It can swim faster than 40 miles per hour. A blue shark swims fastest when it is hunting for food.

A whale shark is 11 times bigger than a human.

The whale shark is the biggest shark. A whale shark can grow to be 15 metres long. That's longer than a bus!

Shark Facts

Some sharks live
more than 100 years.

Some sharks
glow in the
dark.

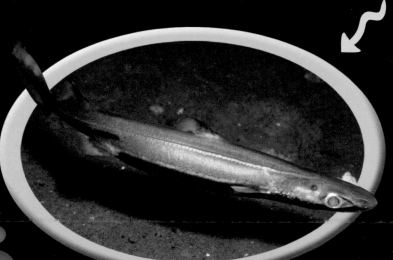

Hammerhead sharks can see nearly all the way around their head.

Sharks can lose up to 30,000 teeth in their life.

The Greenland shark is one of the slowest sharks.

Index

Bones 4, 5

Cartilage 4

Eggs 5, 7

Fins 4, 5, 11, 14

Food 6, 13, 20

Gills 4, 5

Pups 6

Scales 4, 5

Schools 12

Teeth. 8, 14, 23